From Japan:

Graphic design from Japan, compiled and published by Counter-Print

First published in 2015 © Counter-Print
Reprinted in 2017, 2018, 2020
ISBN 978-0-9570816-5-9 Designed by Jon Dowling & Céline Leterme
www.counter-print.co.uk

With special thanks to all the contributors.

Japan boasts a culture that prides itself on harmony, balance and exquisite design.

An island nation lying off the east coast of Asia, with over 127 million inhabitants, Japan saw rapid industrial development throughout the course of the 20th century. This was a major testament to the energy and willpower of the Japanese people, given that it had remained largely isolated until the middle of the 19th century.

During the postwar period of rapid industrial expansion the country also experienced an assimilation of western influences and the problem facing the Japanese graphic designer at this time was how to retain national traditions while incorporating new ideas from beyond their shores. Japan has a strong legacy of design from this period and the work of designers such as Ryuichi Yamashiro, Yusaku Kamekura and Tadanori Yokoo in the 1960's managed to achieve a balance between tradition and modernity which set a benchmark for Japanese graphic design and has gone on to influence many contemporary Japanese designers in this field.

Japanese graphic design today is unique in that it unites traditional and modern aspects of design which can manifest itself in the same designer sometimes creating designs that are extremely traditional and at other times highly modern. No Japanese designer, however, seems to feel the slightest sense of contradiction in this phenomenon.

Japanese design itself is a discipline often full of contradiction. The ancient and modern, simplicity and splendour, eastern and western, handcrafted and mass produced, print and pixel. Past, present and future come together to create an exciting visual mix that is stimulating, energetic and strangely liberating. Much like a trip to Japan itself, where one gets the feeling that modernity is often no more than skin deep. Below, are deep roots of tradition.

Like many European graphic designers, my admiration for Japanese visual culture has instilled in me an enthusiasm for this subject matter. What I notice is a shared desire to communicate ideas and values in the most visually compelling way possible. What I admire, is a delicacy of detail, a fineness of form, a refinement of aesthetics and a collective output that suggests functionalism does not have to be visually arid. →

The influence of Japanese art on western creativity is commonplace and well documented. For instance, great artists such as Van Gogh, Gauguin and Lautrec were undoubtedly influenced by the Japanese print. This influence is manifested not only in the simplicity and general composition but, in Lautrec's case, even his signature, which calls to mind a Japanese letterform.

The Japanese affinity with the practice of creating trademarks is ingrained within their culture and can be attributed, in part, to a longstanding relationship with similar practices. The simple, concentrated and direct visual language of the 'mon' (a family symbol or crest) is part of the fabric of Japanese culture and an important inspiration for the Japanese graphic designer. Dating back to the 12th century, these simplified designs contained within a circle were applied to all belongings and worn on clothing, each Japanese family having its own individual crest.

Some traditions, although ancient, still discretely govern design and much of life in Japan and this is pleasing to witness in a time of such change within our industry.

We have recently experienced one of the most important turning points in graphic design. The internet has had an enormous impact on the transference of ideas between designers and has helped to instigate collaboration between different design communities. Similarly, the advent of new computer technologies has changed the course of graphic design, blurring boundaries between cultures and disciplines.

Corporate identity, as a language understood by all, has seen the logo traverse national boundaries and the spread of information and internationalisation have begun to show their effects in the world of design, where it is often not possible to distinguish the origin of a company's work. However, the nostalgist in me would like to see trademarks and logotypes themselves retaining cultural value and this book is an attempt to present the most progressive graphic design of Japan to an international audience, offering a breath of the country, culture and age.

Finally, I would like to take this opportunity to express my heartfelt thanks to the many people who cooperated in the publication of this book.

Jon Dowling
Counter-Print

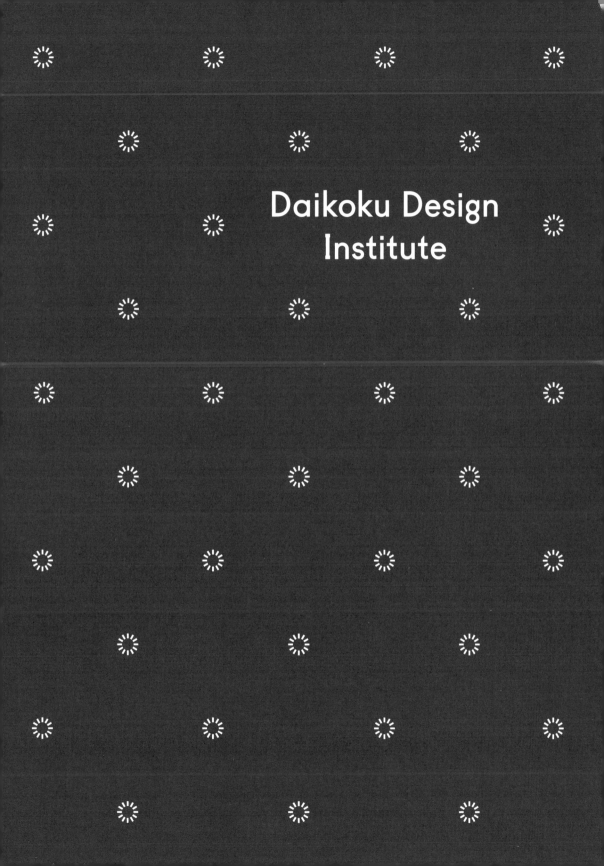

Daikoku Design
Institute

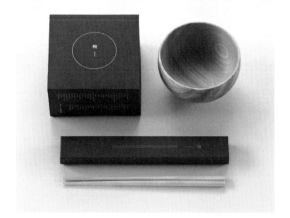

Arishiro Dougu-ten
—————
Packaging design for
a craft-based company
2014

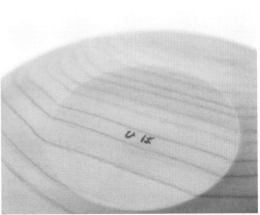

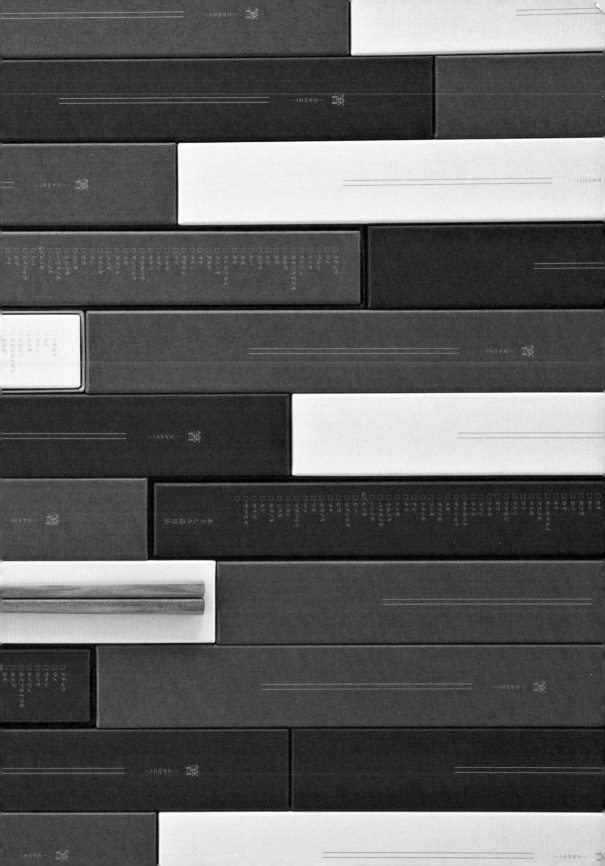

箱根 is
Dream Museum

小田急ロマンスカーと
箱根フリーパスでめぐる。

 100展

**2013
3.9(土)-
3.31(日)**

99体のひみつ道具を持ったドラえもんと元祖ドラえもん1体を
箱根エリア・小田急新宿駅で日本初公開。

フィギュアに付いている2次元コードから、ドラえもんの「ひみつ道具」を集めよう！
[ひみつ道具でかなえたい、あなたの夢を募集中。夢をシェアしよう。] 詳しくは、ホームページ・パンフレットをご覧ください。

| 箱ドラ100 | 検索 |

 映画ドラえもん のび太のひみつ道具博物館 2013 3.9(土)大公開！

Odakyu Electric Railway
Poster for an exhibition
of 100 Doraemons
2013

→
Musashino Art University

Brochures for Musashino
Art University
2011

武蔵野美術大学

2011

JAPANESE PA
SCULPTURE, S
INDUSTRIAL, &

試験問題集

INTING. PRINTMAKING.
MMUNICATION DESIGN.
ND CRAFT DESIGN.

2012年度 入学試験ガイド

■ 一般入学試験
■ 公募制推薦入学試験
■ 外国人留学生特別入学試験
■ 帰国生特別入学試験
■ 3年次編入学試験

謹賀新年2013

Musashino Art University

Musashino Art University
—————————————
New Year's card for
Musashino Art University
2013

→
Kiyosato Shouchu Office
—————————————
Poster for a liquor brand
2013

ARCHITECT KUMA KENGO
HOKKAIDO 北海道
K.KUMA × T.SUZUKI TALK SHOW
KIYO-SATO
2013.6.22(SUN)17:00-19:00

隈研吾 清里

隈研吾氏の本の販売を行います

~ユニークな場所の力を生かせるのは地方~
「建築家隈研吾と清里町の魅力を探る」

日時 | 2013年6月22日(土)17:00~19:00　場所 | 生涯学習総合センター(小ホール)

講師 | 隈研吾(隈研吾建築都市設計事務所代表)　鈴木輝隆(聞き手／江戸川大学社会学部教授)

入場料 | 無料(入場希望の方は、6月18日(火)までに電話などで申し込みください)

主催 | 清里町・清里町教育委員会　申し込み・問い合せ | 清里町生涯学習総合センター　TEL.0152-25-2005　FAX.0152-22-4020

交流会 | 講演会終了後、隈さんを囲んでの交流会を開催しますので、こちらにも是非参加ください(参加費500円)

Odakyu Electric Railway
Poster & timetable design
for a railway
2013

Nendo

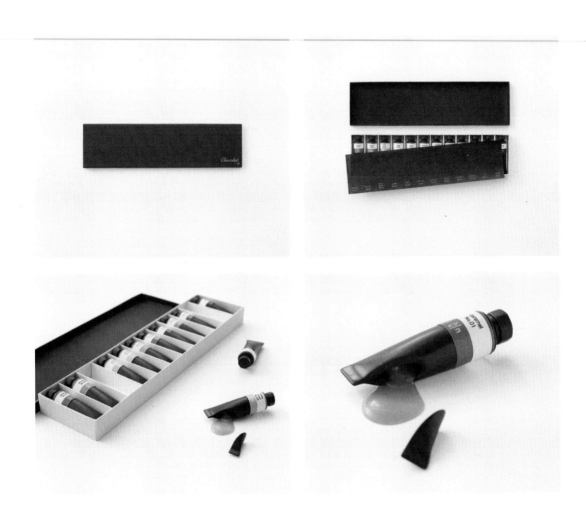

Chocolate-Paint

Chocolate design & packaging

2013

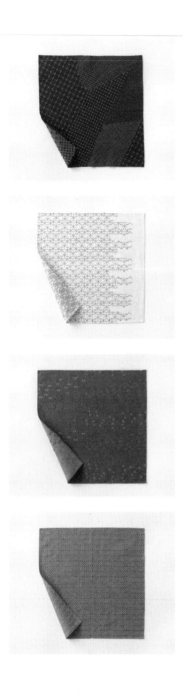

Hosoo
Textile patterns for weaving house
2014

Sekinoichi
Bottle design for coffee beer
2013

Häagen-Dazs
'Village' ice cream cake
for Häagen-Dazs
2014

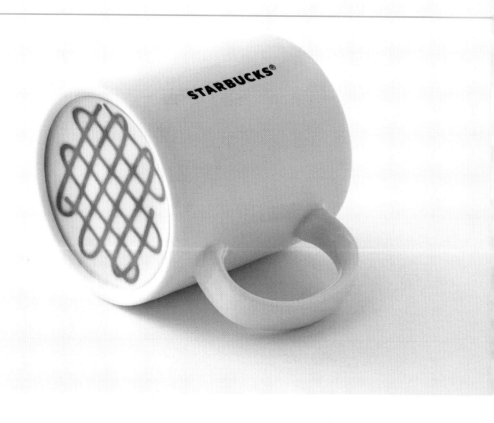

Starbucks

Americano, latte & caramel
macchiato mug graphics
2014

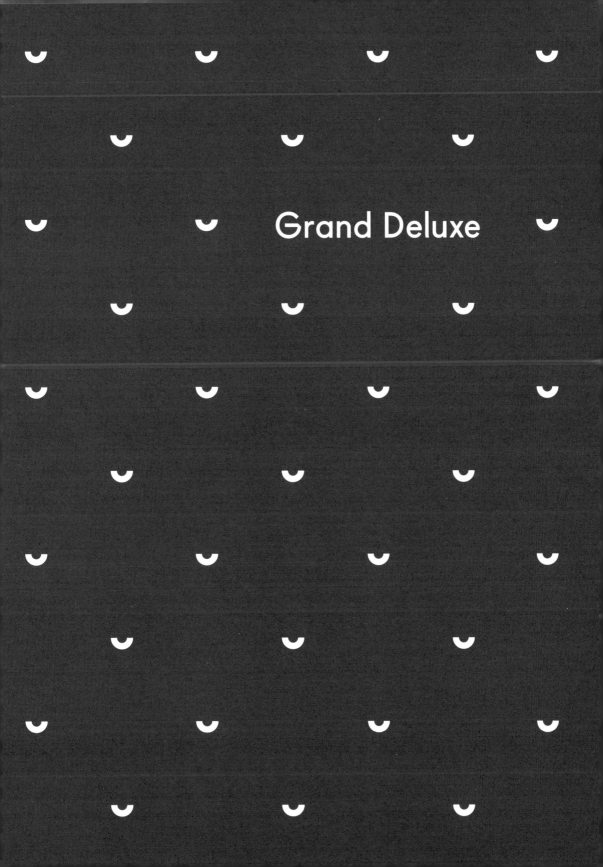
Grand Deluxe

Colorsville Co., Ltd.

Packaging design for fashion brand
2013 – 2014

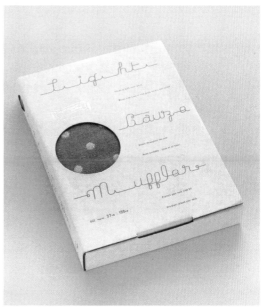

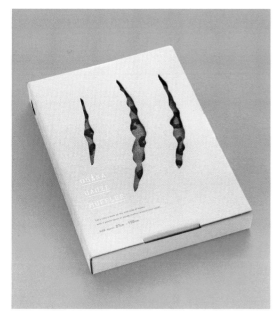

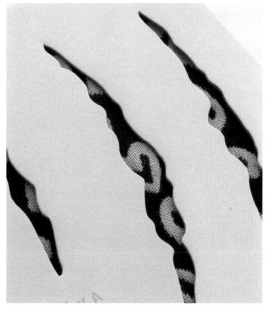

Good Field

Packaging design for
Japanese restaurant
2011 — 2012

Eiko Shuzo

Packaging design for drinks
manufacturer
2010

Himari

Packaging design for
bakery & shop
2012

Zokkon Shikoku

Branding for drinks
manufacturer
2010

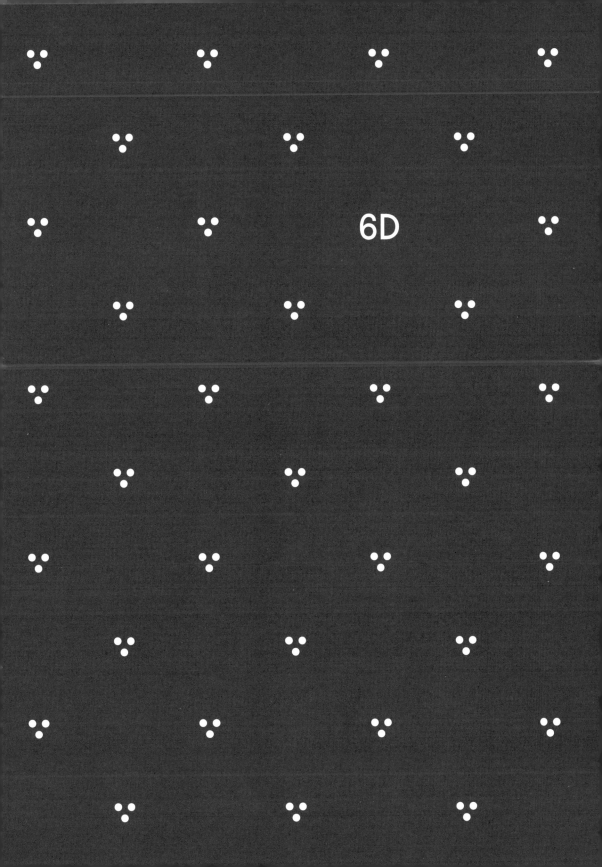

6D

Yuuki Sawaya
Branding for crafters of
high-class pongee silk cloth
2014

TAKEO Co., Ltd.

Branding & collateral
for paper merchants
2013

Kamiwaza Award

http://www.tt-paper.co.jp/kamiwaza

「紙」のもつあたたかさ、しなやかさ、微妙な色合い、
特に意識はしないが、そばにあるとはっとする感覚。
「紙」という素材から創造される夢の中のような世界に親しみ、楽しんでください。
「紙わざ大賞」は「紙」を使用し、自由な発想での創作をテーマとした、
ペーパーアートのコンペティションです。
この度、全国よりご応募いただきました数々の作品の中で、
厳選なる審査により選ばれた作品を紹介いたします。
「紙」から作られた作品達をご覧いただき、
作品より発信される、「紙」の魅力、「紙」の可能性を存分に感じてください。

TOKUSHU
TOKAI
PAPER

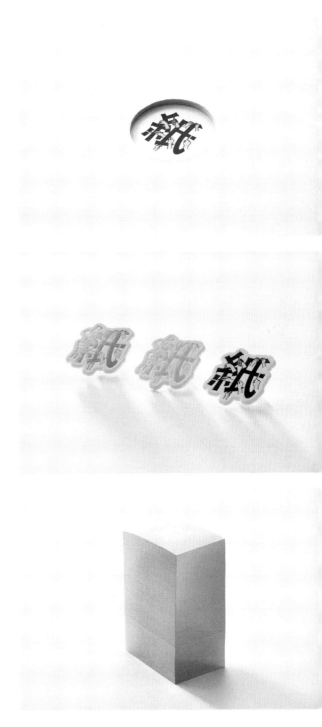

Tokushu Tokai Paper Co., Ltd.

Branding for paper merchants
2013

JA MINDS FARM

Ja Minds Farm
Branding for an agricultural
cooperative
2013

Hand in Hand
_____
Branding for animal welfare
association centered in
Asahikawa, Hokkaido
2013

Hand In Hand

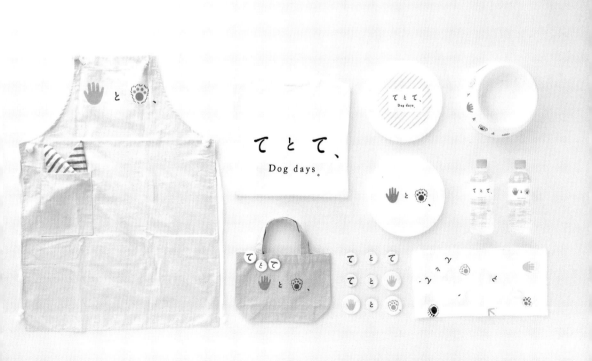

Lacue Co.,Ltd.

Lacue Co., Ltd.
Branding for lettuce farm
in Nagano
2010

Hisamatsuyu
Branding & signage for public
bath house
2014

→

Mitamachi Momonoki
Branding for a Chinese restaurant
2011

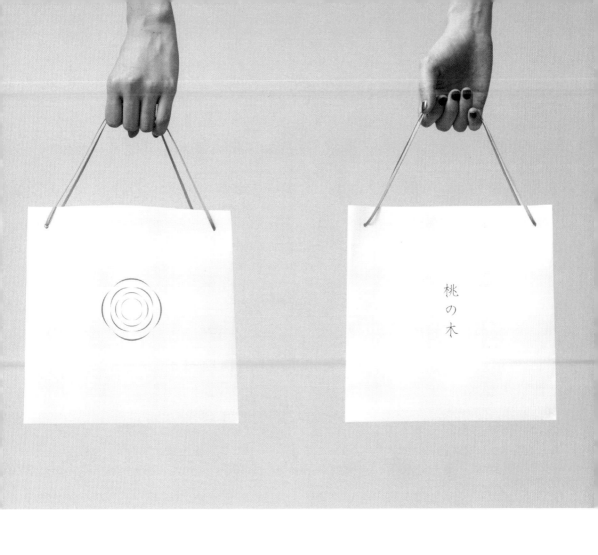

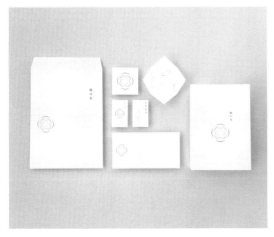

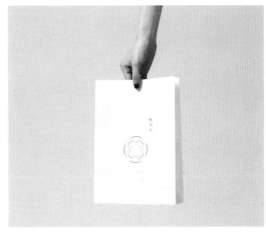

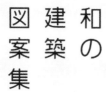
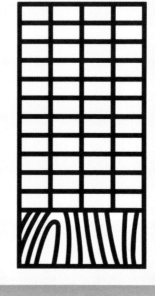

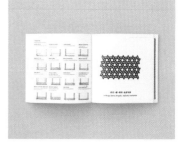

Kenchiku Shiryo Kenkyusha
Co., Ltd.
Book design for publisher
specialising in titles for the
construction industry
2014

The Simple Society

Photography
Yoma Funabashi

Kumakuma-en

Wayfinding system for the Brown
Bear House at the Kumakuma-en
bear zoo in Kita-Akita, Japan
2014

くまくま園のちず
BEAR GARDEN MAP

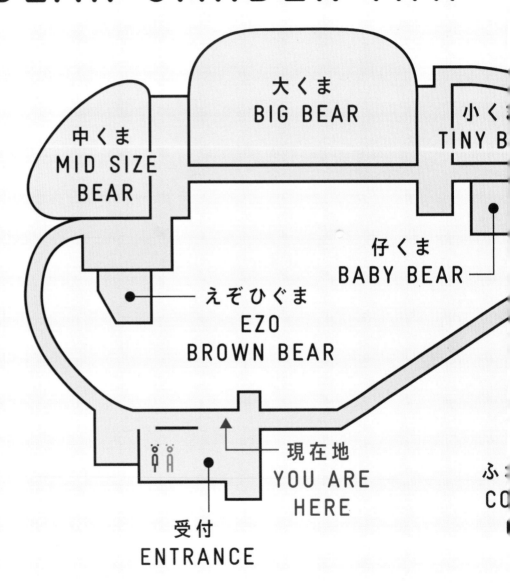

中くま
MID SIZE
BEAR

大くま
BIG BEAR

小く
TINY B

仔くま
BABY BEAR

えぞひぐま
EZO
BROWN BEAR

現在地
YOU ARE
HERE

受付
ENTRANCE

ふ
CO

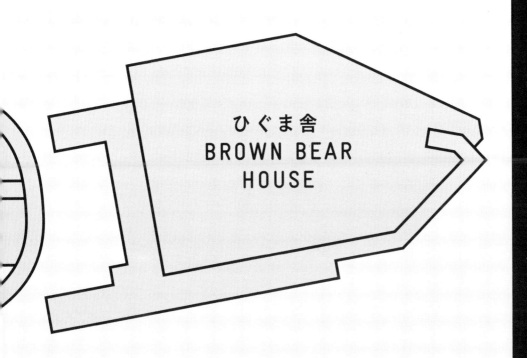

ひぐま舎
BROWN BEAR
HOUSE

い広場
UNITY
DEN

見学されるみなさまへ

※ 「くまのエサ」以外のものを
　投げ込まないでください。
※ フェンスには
　絶対に登らないでください。

シンプル

Photography
Shota Nakamura & Taru Happonen

The Simple Society
& Café Newport
Bag designed for use at
the ZENGOTEN exhibition
2014

フィンランドのくらしとデザイン

ムーミンが住む森の生活展

2012年 4月7日（土）── 6月3日（日）　休館日 5月14日（月）

開館時間　4月7日-5月31日 9:30-17:00　入館16:30まで　6月1日-6月3日 9:00-18:00　入館17:30まで

入場料　一般 1200（1000）円、高大生 700（600）円、小中生 300（200）円
※（　）内は前売および20名以上の団体料金　※心身に障がいがある方と付添者1名は無料
※小・中・特別支援学校の児童生徒及び引率者が、学校教育活動として観覧する場合は無料

主　催　フィンランドのくらしとデザイン展実行委員会（青森県立美術館、青森朝日放送、
　　　　青森県観光連盟、あおもりデザイン協会、あおもりインテリアコーディネーター倶楽部）
協　賛　株式会社千葉工業
後　援　フィンランド大使館、フィンランドセンター、東奥日報社、陸奥新報社、デーリー東北新聞社
協　力　フィンエアー、社団法人日本フィンランド協会、小熊フィンランド協会、Artek、Iittala、
　　　　Marimekko Corporation、弘前大学北日本新エネルギー研究所、青森県菓子工業組合、
　　　　青森市タクシー協会、深浦町
企　画・運営協力　株式会社キュレイターズ　　企画協力　宇都宮美術館
お問合先　フィンランドのくらしとデザイン展実行委員会（青森県立美術館内）
　　　　〒038-0021 青森市安田字近野185
　　　　TEL 017-783-3000　www.aomori-museum.jp

前売券発売所：ローソンチケット（Lコード24816）、チケットぴあ（サークルKサンクス、セブンイレ
ブン等「Pコード756-015」）、サンロード青森、イトーヨーカドー青森店・弘前店、さくら野百貨店
青森店・弘前店・八戸店、三春屋、弘大生協、成田本店しまや店Fax、紀伊國屋書店青森店、県庁生協・
青森県民生協、青森市勤労者互助会、青森市文化会館、青森県立美術館ミュージアムショップ

展覧会特設ウェブサイト
www.finland-design.com

 青森県立美術館
AOMORI MUSEUM OF ART

Aomori Museum of Art

Identity for the exhibition
'Design and Lifestyle of Finland'
2012

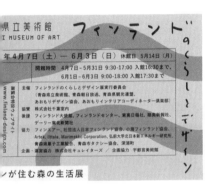

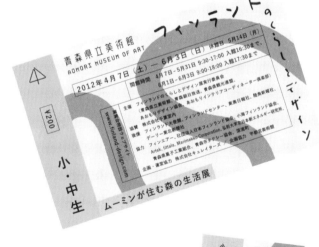

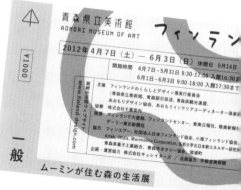

飛騨の森を
いかす割箸

飛ぶように速い馬が駆けたとも
山脈の襞とも、その名が由来される飛騨は
面積の九割以上が森林で覆われている木の国です
木を間引き、森に光を通す「間伐」は
豊かな森を育むために欠かせません
この割箸は飛騨の森の間伐材で作られています

原材料：飛騨杉（間伐材）
製造：飛騨製箸
企画販売：ワリバシカンパニー
warebashi.com

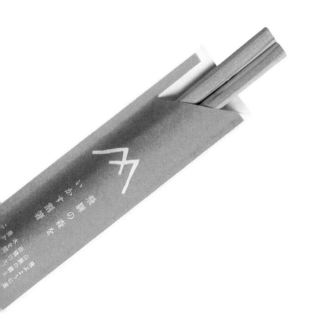

City of Hida
Sleeves to promote chopsticks
made from local sustainable timber
2011

→

m-lab, Tokyo University of Art
'At this Juncture' exhibition poster
2011

えらび なさい
Choose

The choice is not limited to just A or B
選択肢は「A」か「B」だけとは限らない

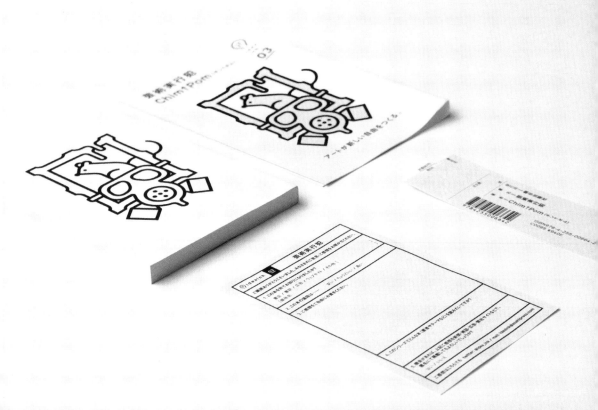

Ideaink for Asahi Press
Book design for publisher
Asahi Press
2012

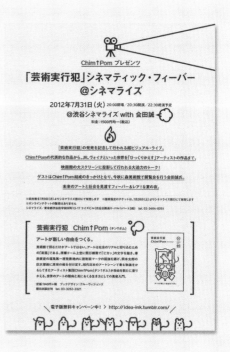

→

Tokyo Metropolitan Art Museum,
Suntory Museum, APT International

Exhibition, poster and book
design for 'Eames Design, Charles
& Ray Eames'

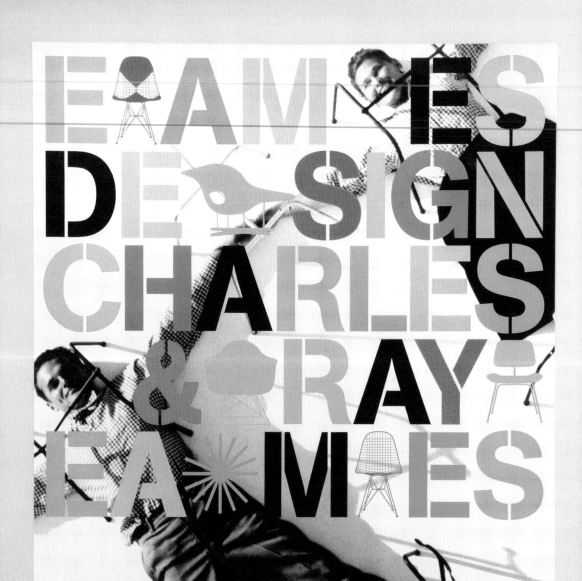

イームズ・デザイン展 | 2001.8.10（金）→9.30（日）東京都美術館 Tokyo Metropolitan Art Museum

主催：東京都美術館、読売新聞社／特別後援：イームズ・オフィス／後援：アメリカ大使館、（社）日本産業デザイン振興会、日本建築家協会、日本グラフィックデザイナー協会、（社）日本インテリアデザイナー協会、（社）日本インダストリアルデザイナー協会、（社）日本ディスプレイデザイン協会、日本デザイン学会、京都デザイン交流協会／協賛・協力：ハーマンミラージャパン、インター・オフィス、日本アイ・ビー・エム、資生堂、ビームス、日本航空／企画：アプトインターナショナル／構成：マイスター・大日本印刷アイ／会場デザイン：武松幸治＋E.P.A／グラフィックデザイン：グルーヴィジョンズ

入場料：一般1200円、学生1000円、小・中・高生600円／お問い合わせ：東京都美術館・上野　ハローダイヤル03-3823-6921（代表）／ http://www.eames-design.net

A-Factory
Branding for JRE-ABC Co., Ltd.
a commercial facility
management company
2010

→

Dentsu Tec, Tokyo Metro
Poster for Tokyo Marathon
2009

すべての人に、東京を走る「楽しさ」を。

TOKYO
MARATHON
2009
3.22(SUN) 9:05 START

東京を走らせる力
東京メトロ
www.tokyometro.jp

東京メトロは東京マラソン2009を応援しています。

Shunsuke
Satake

3.5m

Nishi Ward Office,
Osaka City, Japan
Tsunami warning signs for
Ward Office
2014

↑

浸水 どうぶつものさし
しんすい

キリンは首の高さで 約3.5m
くび　　たか　　　　　　　やく　メートル

成長したキリンが立った状態で地面から首までの高さを示しています。個体差はありますが平均的な数値です。

南海トラフ巨大地震が起こった場合
なんかい　　　きょだいじしん　お　　　　ばあい

周辺は 約3.5m 浸水する可能性があります
しゅうへん　やく　メートル　しんすい　　　　かのうせい

大阪市 西区役所 （平成25年8月時点）

World Animals
Self-initiated illustrations
2012

→

Nikkosha Co., Ltd.
Summer greetings posters
for a printer
2012 – 2013

暑中お見舞い申し上げます

連日の猛暑が続いていますが、お変わりございませんか。
おかげさまで私どもは、元気に過ごしております。
時節柄、ご自愛のほどお祈り申し上げます。

〒550-0004
大阪市西区靱本町1丁目5番6号　本町辰巳マンション401
TEL／FAX　06-1234-5678

日　向　太　郎・花　子

E-mail sample@aisatsujo.com

暑中お見舞い
申し上げます

連日の猛暑が続いていますが、お変わり
ございませんか。
おかげさまで私どもは、元気に過ごして
おります。時節柄、ご自愛のほどお祈り
申し上げます。

〒五五〇-〇〇〇四
大阪市西区靱本町一丁目五番六号
本町辰巳マンション四〇一
電話　〇六-一二三四-五六七八
E-mail sample@aisatsujo.com

日向　太郎　　花子

Animal Children
Self-initiated illustrations
2011

→
Design & Creative Center Kobe

Creative workshop Chibikkobe

2014

子どものまちで
つくろう！遊ぼう！
お仕事しよう！

みんな、集まれ

CREATIVE WORKSHOP
ちびっこうべ2014
—— 子どものまちは、神戸の未来。——
2014年10月11日(土)▶26日(日)

入場無料 申し込み不要 ※10月25日(土)をのぞく

※一部、有料プログラムがあります。
※来場者多数の場合、安全確保のために入場制限することがあります。

「ちびっこうべ」は、神戸の子どもたちと
クリエイターがいっしょにつくる、夢のまち。
プロの知識や技を楽しく学んで、買い物をしたり、
仕事をしたり、ものづくりが体験できます。

ところ デザイン・クリエイティブセンター神戸

対 象 小学3年生〜中学3年生
※「子どもエリア」には、中学生以下のお子さまのみ入場できます。

子どものまちオープン！
10月12日(日)13日(月/祝)
18日(土)19日(日)
12:30から17:00まで
神戸の「食」をテーマにした15の「ユメミセ」の
ほか、いろんなショップやお仕事、
ものづくりを体験できるコーナーが！

オープニングイベント&ユメミセ発表会
10月11日(土) 11:30から15:30まで
子どもたちがまちを紹介する、スペシャルイベントを開催！
午後からは「ユメミセ」のお披露目も。この日は大人も
「子どもエリア」に入場できます。
※見学のみ。ワークショップはございません。

子どものまち展示
10月15日(水)〜17日(金)
21日(火)〜26日(日) 11:00から19:00まで
この日は大人も自由に、子どものまち
を見学できます。

クロージングトーク&パーティ
10月25日(土) 19:00から21:30まで
要申し込み 定員 150名
KIITOウェブサイトから
お申し込みください。
ひと晩だけ、子どものまちが大人のまちに！ちびっ
こうべに参加した思い出を語り合うひとときです。

CREATIVE WORKSHOP ちびっこうべ 2014 主催：デザイン・クリエイティブセンター神戸 協力：神戸芸術工科大学、神戸・三宮センター街
後援：朝日新聞社、NHK神戸放送局、MBS、関西テレビ放送、Kiss FM KOBE、神戸市教育委員会、神戸商工会議所、神戸新聞社、産経新聞社、
サンテレビジョン、日本経済新聞社大阪本社、毎日新聞神戸支局、読売新聞神戸総局、読売テレビ、ラジオ関西

KII+O:
デザイン・クリエイティブセンター神戸 (KIITO)
〒651-0082 神戸市中央区小野浜町1-4 TEL 078-325-2235

http://kiito.jp

City of Design
KOBE

ちびっこうべ
CREATIVE WORK SHOP
CHIBIKKOBE

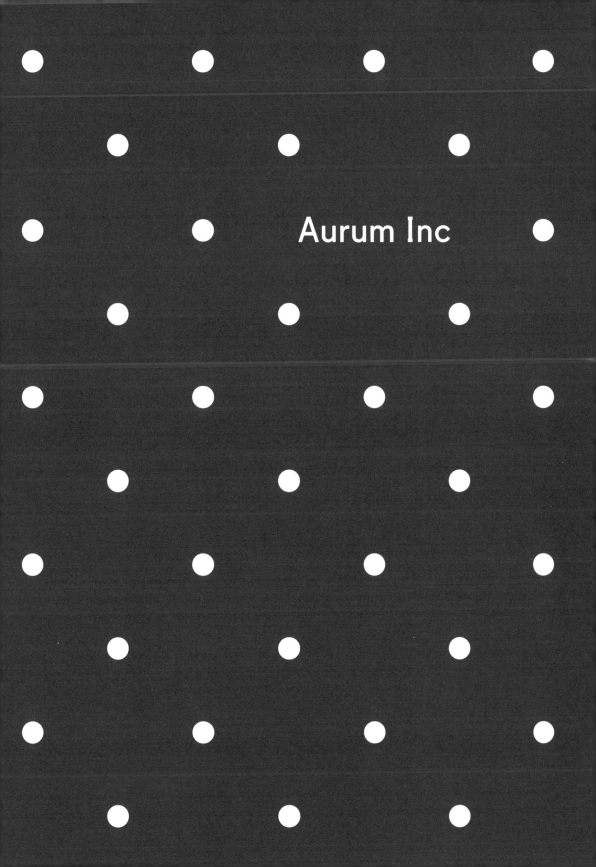

Aurum Inc

Nakameguro Lounge
Café & restaurant branding
for A Style Works
2009

Photography
Kei Tanaka

Photography
Kei Tanaka

Franx Ltd.
Café & restaurant branding
for Chabi
2010

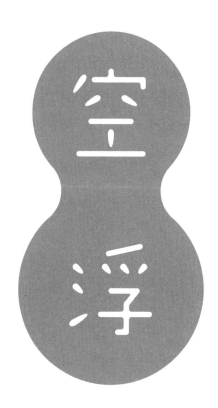

Sorauki
Strawberry
Garden

Sorauki Strawberry Garden

Branding for a strawberry farm

2009

Photography
Kei Tanaka

Sorauki Strawberry Garden

Branding for a strawberry farm
2009

Photography

Kei Tanaka

→

Muza Kawasaki Symphony Hall

Poster for Muza New Year concert
2013

MUZA ニューイヤーコンサート 2014

MUZA
KAWASAKI
SYMPHONY HALL

聴き初めは、ミューザで。

ヴァイオリン
グレブ・ニキティン
Gleb Nikitin, Violin

東京交響楽団室内合奏団
Tokyo Symphony Chamber Orchestra

♪ヴィヴァルディ：ヴァイオリン協奏曲集「四季」より 春、冬
♪J.S.バッハ：ヴァイオリン協奏曲第1番 ホ短調
♪チャイコフスキー：弦楽セレナーデ
♪クライスラー：愛の喜び、愛の悲しみ、美しきロスマリン 他

2014年1月3日(金) 14:00開演(13:30開場)
会場＝ミューザ川崎シンフォニーホール

| チケット料金 | 全席指定：¥3,000（友の会会員 ¥2,700） |
| チケット発売日 | 一般：9月24日(火)／Web会員先行：9月17日(火)／友の会：9月14日(土) |

主催＝ミューザ川崎シンフォニーホール（川崎市文化財団グループ）

Nakano
Design Office

SFIDA Football
Logo & visual identity for Imio
2008

2008年11月15日(土)
▼
2009年2月1日(日)
開館時間:10:00～17:00(入場は16:30まで)
休館日:月曜日(祝日の場合は翌日)、
12月29日～1月3日

第4回府中ビエンナーレ

同時開催:
袴田京太朗 公開制作
「1000層」

トゥルー・カラーズ

雨宮庸介　今津正　原高史　武藤努　村山留里子　横内賢太郎　渡辺豊

色 を め ぐ る 冒 険

The 4th Fuchu Biennial True Colors

料金: 一般600(480)円、高校・大学生300(240)円、
小・中学生150(120)円
( )内は20名以上の団体料金
未就学児および障害者手帳等をお持ちの方は無料、
府中市内の小・中学生は
「学びのパスポート」で無料

府中市美術館
Fuchu Art Museum
〒183-0001 東京都府中市浅間町1-3
ハローダイヤル:
03-5777-8600
http://www.city.fuchu.tokyo.jp/art/

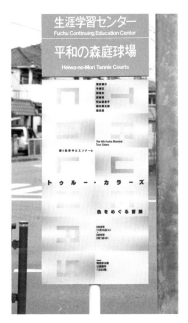

Fuchu Art Museum

Collaborative cover, poster
& signage with media artist,
Tsutomu Muto for Art Museum
2008

→

Axis Gallery

Poster designed for the 'More
Trees' exhibition, promoting forest
preservation
2010

more trees 展

森を感じる12日間

10.27 wed ▶ **11.7** sun

協力：高知県中土佐町、コエドビール、有限会社サイン技研、株式会社牡丹屋、株式会社丹青社、中越パルプ工業株式会社、トムス・ガーデン株式会社、飛騨産業株式会社、株式会社プレディックグリーン、マックスレイ株式会社、宮崎県森林組合連合会、山本企画工芸株式会社（五十音順）

11:00→19:00 ● 最終日は17:00まで ● 入場料：無料
会場：アクシスギャラリー他 アクシスビル内 ● 東京都港区六本木 5-17-1 ● 03-5575-8655
主催／企画：more trees ＋アクシスギャラリー
http://www.more-trees.org ● http://www.axisinc.co.jp

more **Trees**　AXIS GALLERY

MR Design

CGB
Refuse sacks for Fuji
Television Network
2005

Sushi Memo Block

Memo block for 'nico' range
2002 – 2013

Hinoki Memo Cube
Memo block for 'nico' range
2002 – 2013

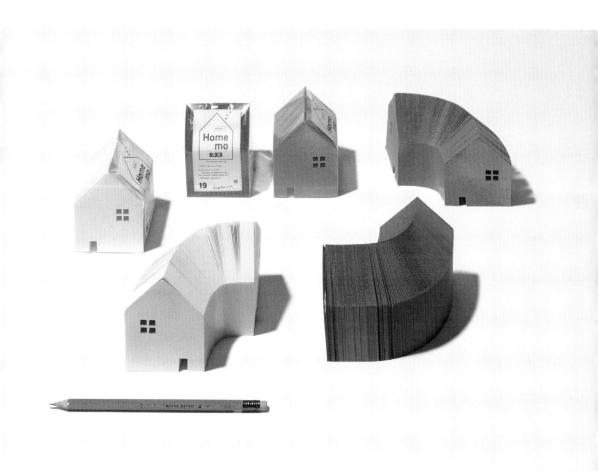

Home Memo Block
Memo block for 'nico' range
2002 – 2013

Commune

Ritaru
—
Branding for coffee shop
2013

Ritaru
—
Branding for coffee shop
2013

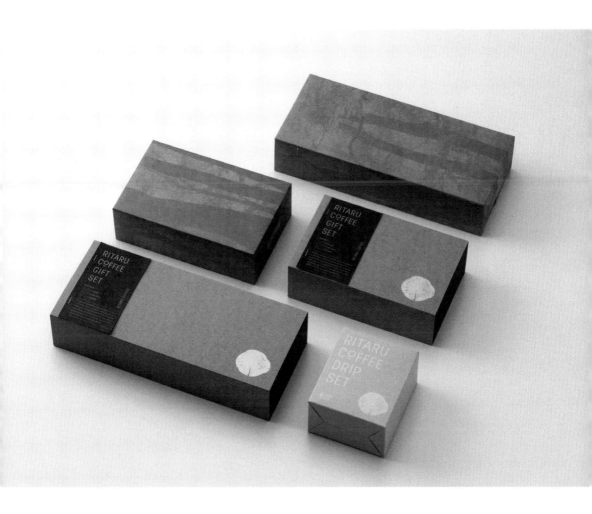

Milkraft

Identity for paper
manufacturing company
2009

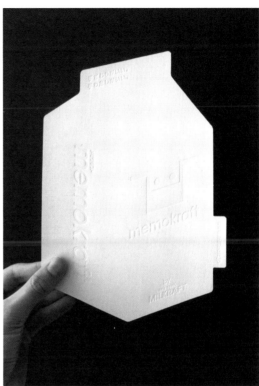

Yuko Ono Sthlm
—————
Branding for Japanese
tea brand
2012

Hirokazu
Matsuda

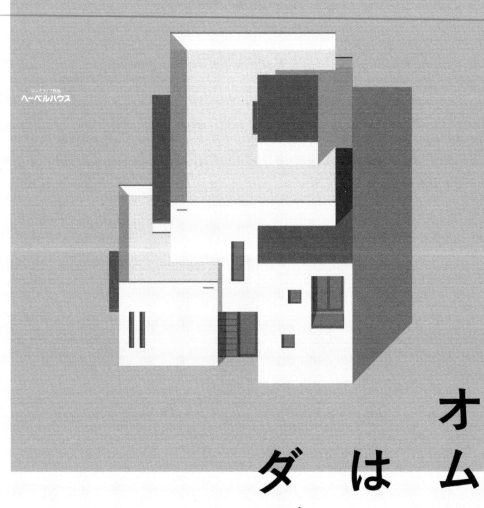

オムツを
はいた
ダデイ。

玄孫
と 住む日が
やってくる。

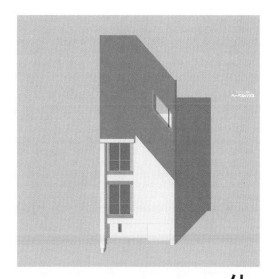

休日
嫁日
姑嫁と
。私とと

80th Mainichi
Advertising Design Award
Design for competition
of newspaper advertising
2012

Hekichi
Business card for art unit
2011

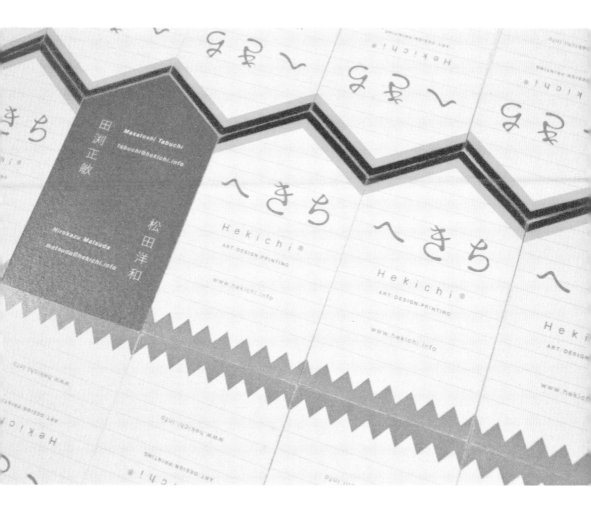

ha
na.
REi

hanarei

demonstration compact disc includes three songs.
01 loft 4'10"/02 gunjyou 4'32"/03 hyperbola 4'00"

HD.001 STEREO ℗©hanarei All Rights Of The Manufacturer And Of The Owner
Of The Recorded Work Reserved. Unauthorized Public Performance,
Broadcasting, Renting And Copying Of This Disc Prohibited. hanarei.

Hanarei
Music sleeve for band
2013

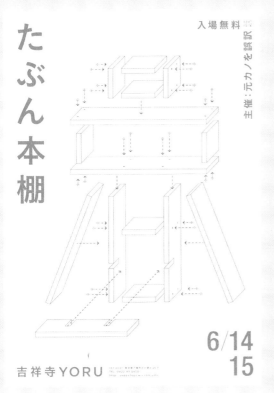

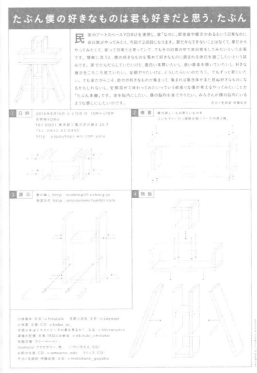

aaAaa
Logo design for fashion brand
2014

Terashima
Design Co.

Day by Day

Poster design for 23rd
anniversary of jazz bar
2006

Terashima Design

Poster design for design office
2010

→
Day by day

Poster design for live jazz
in Shin-Yakushijl
2007

SA PPORO DE SIGN WEEK 2010

MAIN THEME
PARTY

10.28 THU ▶ **11.3** WED

◇ SAPPORO DESIGN AWARD 2010
◇ DESIGN SEMINAR
◇ SAPPORO DESIGN SWEETS 2010
◇ DESIGN EXHIBITION

HYPERLINK "http://www.sapporodesignweek.com"

←

Sapporo Design Week Committee	Growing Home Build	Ikenobo Sapporo
Poster design for Sapporo Design Week	Poster design for Growing Home Build, a house builder	Poster design for cultural organisation, Ikenobo Sapporo
2010	2011	2010

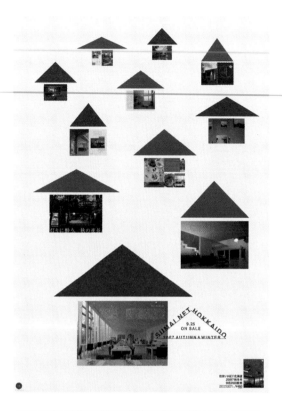

Sumai-net Hokkaido

Autumn poster design for
housing magazine
2007

Sumai-net Hokkaido

Spring poster design for
housing magazine
2008

Japan Graphic Designers
Association Inc.

Poster design for JAGDA
Hokkaido Poster Exhibition
2010

Maru

Umeboshi8
Branding for Kadoya,
a food retailer
2014

Mikan Hachimitsu
Branding for Kadoya,
a food retailer
2014

Silk
Branding for a dry-cleaning shop
2011

www.kinbachimikan.com

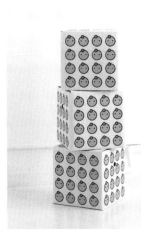
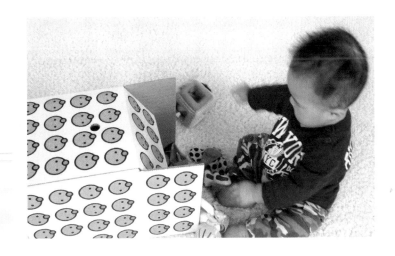

Kinpachi Mikan

Branding for Kadoya,
a food retailer
2014

Sensyukai

Branding for Mammy Rakü,
a mail order company
2014

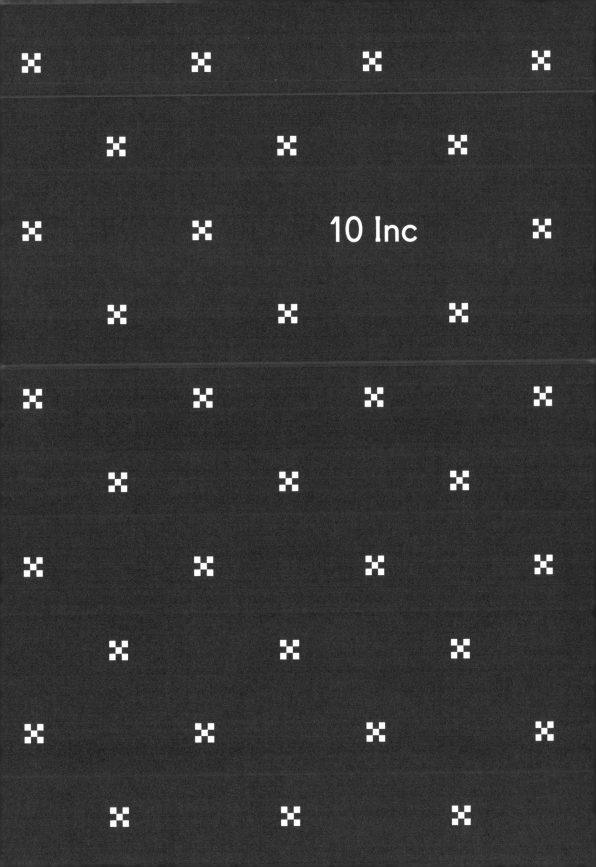

10 Inc

Japan Graphic Designers

Association Inc.

Book & posters for design
association
2009

R.O.U
Department store branding
for Aeon Retail Co., Ltd.
2009 – Present

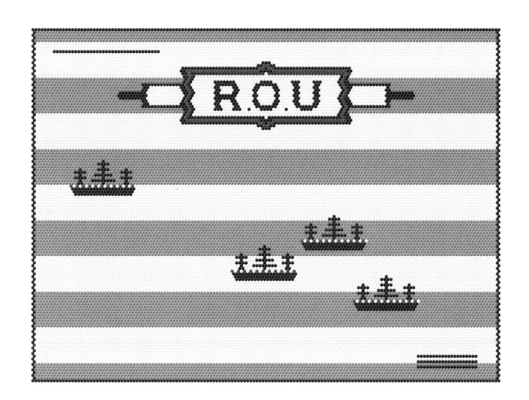

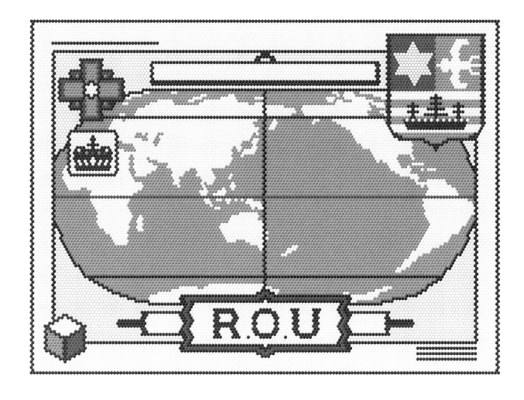

R.O.U
Department store branding
for Aeon Retail Co., Ltd.
2009 – Present

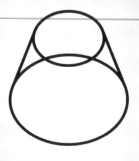

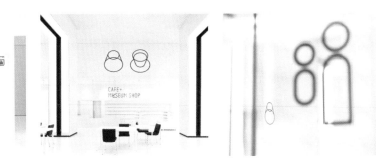

Shiuzoka City Museum of Art
Branding & signage for Art Museum
2009

T Square Design Associates

KOTOHA with Yuica
Packaging for Sei-Plus toiletries
2011

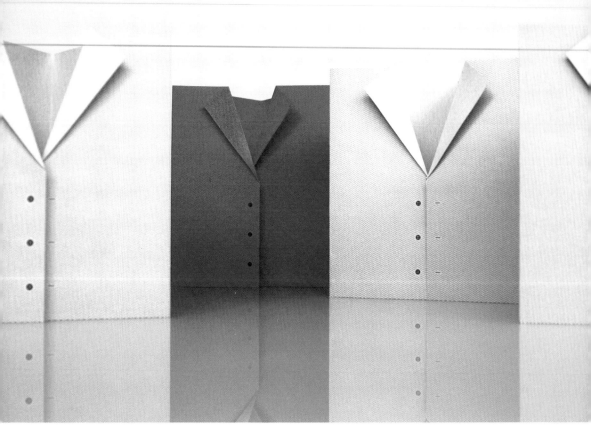

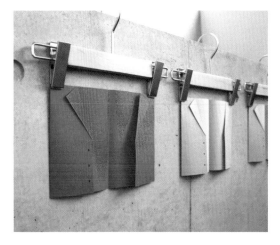

TPO
—
Book jackets for fine paper
distributor Takeo
2011

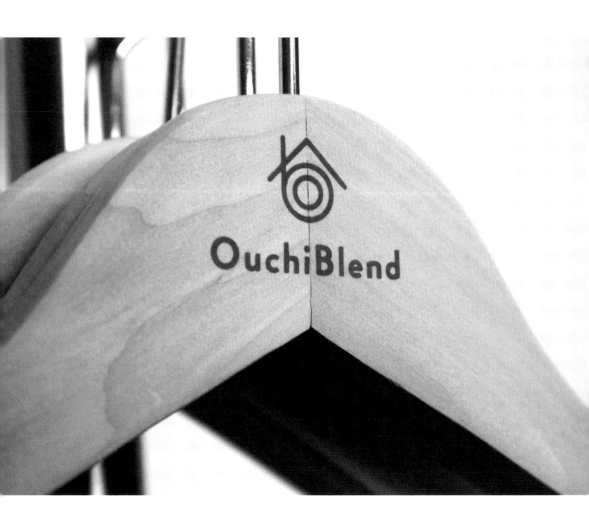

OuchiBlend
Identity for fashion brand
2011

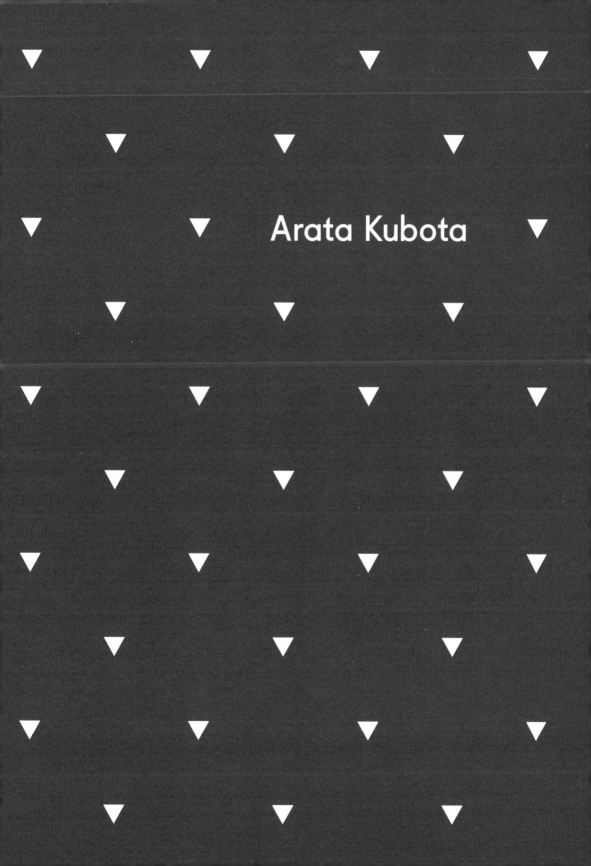

Arata Kubota

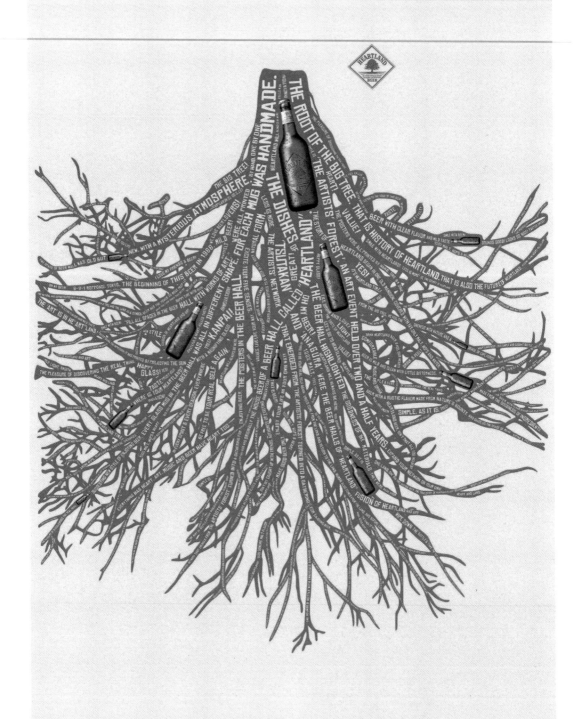

Heartland Beer
————
Advertising for Kirin beer
2012

→
Akiko
————
Poster designs for record
label Ability Muse
2012

Swingy Swingy

akiko
with Cui-CuiSisters

2.May
Release

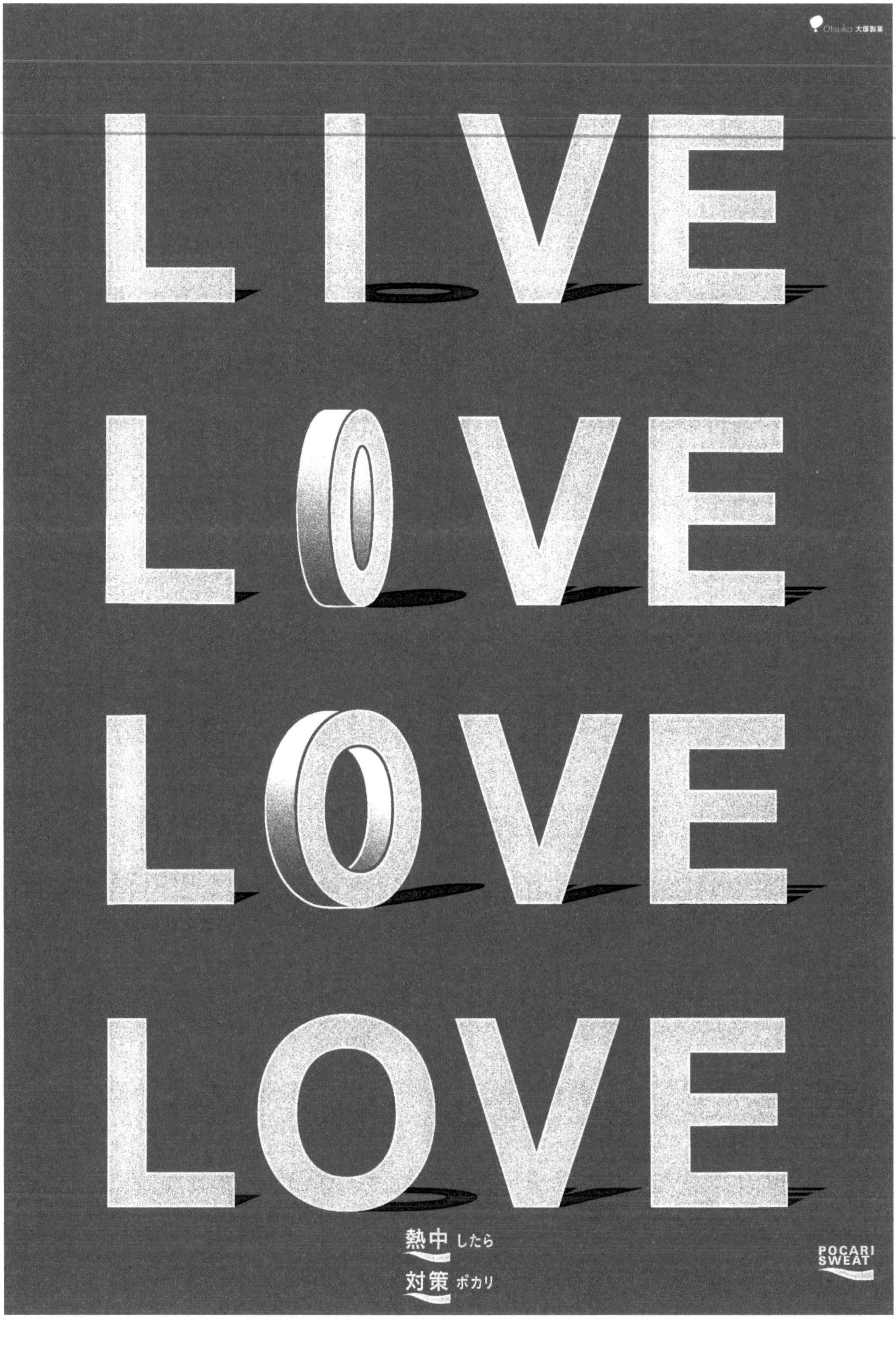

Otsuka 大塚製薬
LIVE
LOVE
LOVE
LOVE
熱中したら
対策ポカリ
POCARI SWEAT

Pocari Sweat
—
Poster designs for drinks
manufacturer Otsuka
2012

→
Tokio Marine Nichido
Posters for Junior Olympic Cup
2014

はじめて会うけど、みんなずっとライバルだった。

東京海上日動

泳ぎつづけた日々の、ラストスパートだ。

東京海上日動

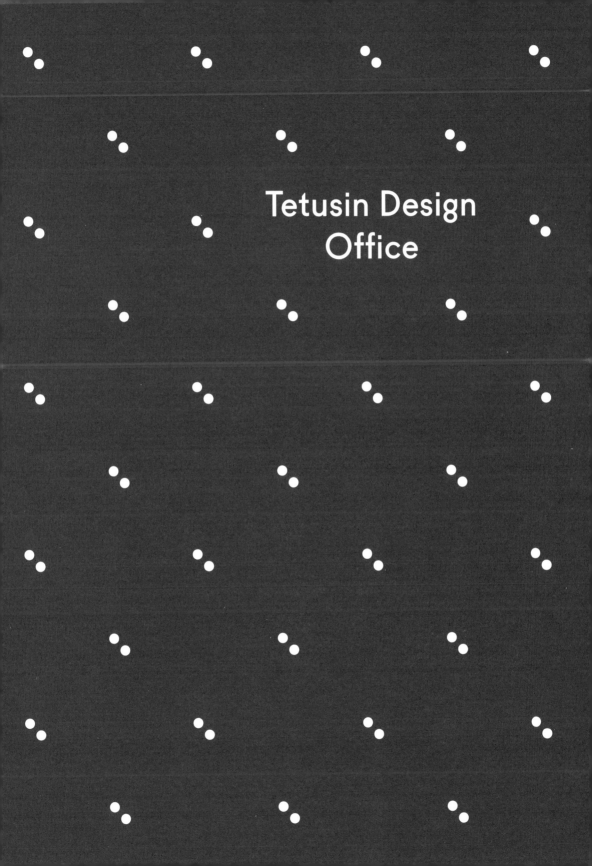

Tetusin Design
Office

La Terra
———
Branding for restaurant
2009

Pizza

La Te

La Terra

Kurashino
—
Branding, signage & interior design
for architect
2012

Photography
Daisuke Ikeda & Hiromasa Ohtsuka

Kurashino

Branding, signage & interior design
for architect
2012

Architect
Kosuke Ariyoshi

Shunmai Shinkan

Packaging design for drinks brand

2012

Daikoku Design Institute daikoku.ndc.co.jp

Nendo nendo.jp

Grand Deluxe grand-deluxe.com

6D 6d-k.com

The Simple Society thesimplesociety.com

Groovisions groovisions.com

Shunsuke Satake naturalpermanent.com

Aurum Inc aurumdesign.info

Nakano Design Office nakano-design.com

MR Design mr-design.jp

Commune commune-inc.jp

Hirokazu Matsuda matsudahirokazu.com

Terashima Design Co. tera-d.net

Maru maruinc.net

10 Inc 10inc.jp

T Square Design Associates t2designassociates.jp

Arata Kubota aratakubota.com

Tetusin Design Office tetusin.com